True IT Maturity

Rethinking IT Management in the Cloud Era

Matthew Murren

AND

Marc T. Shaw

Printed in the United States of America

First Printing, 2014

ISBN 978-1-312-66197-4

True North ITG
16504 9th Ave SE, Suite #203
Mill Creek, WA 98012

www.truenorthitg.com

CONTENTS

Acknowledgements   I

Preface   II

IT Maturity Graphic   IV

Chapter 1 IT, The Thankless Job   1

Chapter 2 Users, Printer Problems, and BYOD   9

Chapter 3 Control, Now You Have It, Now You Don't   13

Chapter 4 Backups – Why Can't They Ever Get This $#!t To Work?   19

Chapter 5 Security – It's An Inside Job!   25

Chapter 7 Cumulous, Nebulous, and Other Clouds   37

Chapter 8 But Weekends Are For More Work, Right?   47

Chapter 9 Right, But Where's My Raise?   54

Chapter 10 Yep, It's Another Gartner Quadrant Discussion 61

ACKNOWLEDGEMENTS

As is the case with any project of broad scope, it would be impossible to bring to fruition without the help of a broad support base. Thanks first of all to our team at True North, who served as sounding boards for the presentation, articulation, and design of the book, not to mention for refining the process of delivering award winning Mature IT services to our many clients over the years.

Ideas have to go through many stages to achieve maturity, and specifically Ted Grandpre and Jordan Shaw have lent their internal and external expertise both in developing solutions to meet client needs, and in identifying a successful mentality for sustaining momentum in IT and IT consulting services.

Our clients have instructed us at every step of the way, whether a solution was successful or not, we've been attentive and learned from the process with invaluable wisdom gleaned from each interaction, refining our approach to Mature IT services.

Thanks to our wives for their patience and our children who keep motivating us to do better.

A special word of thanks to Tina Shaw for her invaluable insights into refining ideas into presentable form and for her keen eye for design, matching the book's concepts with a visual style.

PREFACE

The next big thing. It's here.

Isn't that what we're told, time and time again? From cars to phones to TV commercials, that phrase gets tossed around an awful lot. In IT, it's unavoidable. That's the whole logic behind technology, right? It's always evolving. And from the rise of PCs to the internet to smart phones to cloud computing, our industry does indeed change at a rapid rate. As IT professionals we've got to keep our finger on the pulse at all times, making sure our service offerings stay current, keeping our expertise up to date, and reading market trends. Company goals have to be reexamined quarterly, and services revamped seemingly every six months. To achieve any kind of success in this field, you absolutely have to stay agile, and that means looking ahead at all times. With so many bases to cover, it can be tricky to stay focused. Much as we understand the need for forward thinking and innovation, at True North we firmly believe that one key ingredient to consistent progress is staying true to core principles.

In the pages that follow, we hope to provide some insight into the core principles that deeply shape our decision making at True North. They inform how we assess client network infrastructures and how we advise CEOs who come to us with the stickiest IT problems. We keep them in mind whether consulting with an SMB prospect for the first time or sitting down with the board of a 300 doctor medical facility.

Taken together, they form what we call the IT Maturity Model.

From technology and employee management to organizational turmoil and competitive markets, the IT role can seem like a constantly raging storm. Staying focused on core principles instills confidence and helps maintain clear direction. The idea behind this book is not to tout "the next big thing." We'll let the ad agencies do that. Instead, we want to provide you with a means of seeing clearly, of moving forward in the right frame of mind.

We'd like to outline our IT Maturity Model as a compass to help you find your organization's own true north. We truly hope you benefit from our experience and our time tested approach to navigating business through technology. The ITG at the end of our company name stands for Information Technology Group. In developing robust IT services for over a decade, we know as well as anybody that success in this industry is a collaborative process. Sometimes we need to help guide each other to move forward. We hope this book helps sharpen your decision making and helps increase the value you bring to your team. Enjoy the ride!

Matt Murren
True North ITG
Mill Creek, WA
October, 2014

Infographic: The Maturity Model

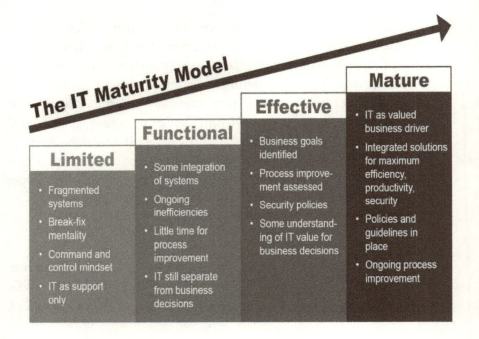

Key

For the skim reader or for those who wish to return to key ideas and exercises quickly, we've provided the following symbols in the text.

 Main idea

 Practical details and examples

 Suggested Exercise

Chapter 1
IT, The Thankless Job

Overworked Much?

It's Friday. It's coming up on 7 pm. Your stomach growls. You haven't had a bite since twelve thirty lunch break. It's getting late, but once again, there's a problem. Another fire to be put out. There've been a lot this week, it seems. In fact, there are a lot every week these days. It's the fourth day in a row you've had to stay late. You stretch your back. You've been sitting for long stretches again, today even more than usual.

How about that gym membership you've been thinking about? Would you even have time? Sure, if you set the alarm for 5:30 am. And that's after you were on call all night. Got to maintain those 24 hour SLAs.

Oh, the humanity!

And let's not even get started on this particular problem tonight, AD issues, two printers, a mouse. You assigned an assistant to fix the printers and mouse on Wednesday, yet here you are, on Friday, whittling away. And if it isn't done on time? Another complaint. And if it is? Well, then things will simply run as expected and everyone will go about their day.

Sound familiar?

IT managers everywhere experience this "high demand/low appreciation" phenomenon, even as they try to balance system management with ticky-tacky end user issues. As the world moves into the cloud and use of mobile devices expands, the sense of entitlement and expectation of smoothly running IT only grows. End users are promised a seamless computing experience across multiple devices, from anywhere. This can cause headaches for IT managers who are used to a security-first mentality, trying to protect the integrity of their local network and making sure everything stays secure first and foremost.

It's a two-edged sword. On the one hand, more complex IT is good for business: as IT pros, our livelihood depends on this very demand for high functioning IT services. The more problems there are to solve, the more work there is for the one solving them. On the other hand, the problems are never ending, and the organizations we serve too often take the demands and intricacies of these problems for granted, understaffing their IT departments and increasing the burden. End users adopt the attitude: "You're the expert. Just fix it." They want access to data and applications with cross-device integration, all with high availability, and don't necessarily appreciate the finer points of what it takes to make it all possible.

Another stressor is the ever-evolving nature of the field itself. As the technology evolves, the discipline becomes more and more specialized. Are your certifications up to date? Are you staying marketable in an unstable job market? Do you have the cloud computing chops? How are your management skills? Where is the market headed? From HP to Microsoft to Amazon, there are not only new product offerings, but also seemingly new rounds of layoffs around every corner. Consolidation, outsourcing, competition in a global job market. These issues can become a black cloud hanging over our daily stressors, of which there are already quite a few.

On Friday nights you might just want to kick back and abide, instead of worrying about a single point of failure, or, say, a malfunctioning mouse connection.

Right. But Is It Working?

By and large, people don't much care about the details of their organization's IT infrastructure, they just want to connect the internet at high speeds, complete their work without much fuss or interruption, and print the occasional document.

Try this. Give an actual description for just one of the troubleshooting solutions you cook up in a given week to one of your organization's rank and file employees when they ask, or when they enter a service ticket and you come calling. Be thorough. Don't forget the documentation piece.

Then, watch their eyes glaze over. You might end up having to chase them down the hall to finish the story.

You may have a comprehensive map of your organization's IT infrastructure swimming around your brain, several layers deep, no less. But if your organization is like most, no one else does. Most organizations and their employees take the how of their IT infrastructure for granted. Security, redundancy, single points of failure, disaster recovery, failover. They don't know and they don't want to know. That's why they hire experts like you to take care of the problem. They just want to type their documents, send their emails, and sneak a peek of their Facebook feed with limited interruptions.

In society in general, we've become accustomed to instant gratification. We're a microwave culture. If there's an obstacle to our activity, we become frustrated. If the accountant bought some accounting software, they expect it to work. After all, they read the glossy cover or listened to the sales rep with the seductive voice, became convinced of the value of its many features, were sold on it, and now, they want to get to work. Drivers? Plug-ins? Updates? Compati-what? Don't bother me with the details. Just make it work.

All too often, IT managers can come to feel like the office whipping boy, underappreciated. Tucked away in the bowels of the office, hidden from daylight, a decided dearth of vitamin D, expected to be available at the drop of a hat to fix any and every problem, many of which are avoidable, not to mention repetitive. The IT industry may categorize them as Tier 1 problems, but the Account Manager simply wants to print out a client contract, and can't. Again. And so you're trotted out. Again. Surviving can take zen-like patience!

You Are Not Alone, Neo!

First off, in enduring these many frustrations, you're not alone (as indicated in the clever sub-header). Studies show a majority of IT managers report burnout as a major occupational hazard. The organization wants to cut costs. You're under pressure to optimize processes, foresee problems, develop policies, and react to both internal organizational changes as well as shifts in the external market. On top of all this, much of our interaction can be with people in the middle of a stressful situation, ready to boil over because something they rely on isn't working for one reason or another.

This can tap into a characteristic that is inherent in many people who go into IT in the first place: problem solving. Frequently, IT managers are people who have a knack for understanding systems and solving problems in life in general. They recognize patterns, identify the main problem, and work to address it. They're proud of this, and take ownership and responsibility of solutions they put in place. IT managers, especially newer ones, can take it personally and internalize whatever daily stress they've been subjected to; they feel responsible for fixing problems and feel frustrated about loose ends. Left unchecked over time, this can cause serious stress manifesting in physical symptoms and, eventually, burnout. Increasing workloads, a rapid rate of change, high pressure environments. If you add difficult company culture on top of this, those that prioritize competition over collaboration, or don't foster a sense of support, for instance, life can become pretty miserable, sometimes for years.

From the internet to self-help books, there is a ton of literature out there to help with these kinds of issues. Some advocate culture change, others constructive confrontation to get all the issues on the table. Others still focus on practical steps toward personal well-being, and might include advice on personal fitness, maintaining a healthy diet, drinking enough water, slowing down to meditate for even 10 minutes a day, repetition of positive phrases, and so on. Some of these can be helpful, some devolve into cultural cliché. We're going a different route here.

Coping strategies can make life more tolerable, but they won't necessarily provide you with an overall schema or mental model to understand your current situation and to plan accordingly. This shift in thinking, this cognitive framework, is what we want to outline in this book. In so doing, we hope to provide a practical means of addressing some of the issues confronting today's IT director.

The IT Maturity Model

There is always a learning and growth component to any job, in any field. We want to suggest an important part of the IT manager's job today is the way they think about their role and the industry in general. Understanding this key component will allow you to make decisions with a more comprehensive picture in mind. There is a shift going on in the role of the IT manager, and it has to be reckoned with, no matter the size of your organization or the length of your tenure in your current position.

With any new technology, there are five stages of adoption. And just in case you've forgotten the official title for stage four, here they are:

1. Innovators
2. Early adopters
3. Early majority
4. Late majority
5. Laggards

We'd like to suggest that these current changes, if not attended to, will leave many in stages four and five either out in the cold, or else frustrated and confused much of the time. If their lack of understanding is recognized by their organization, at the very least they will likely be excluded from major decision-making processes, many of which could have a major impact on them and their department.

What is this mysterious change? For starters, it is the ability to think doubly, a capacity for dual-mindedness. You have to be able to analyze situations from the perspective of both IT *and* business needs at every step. This thinking has to be integrated into organizational decision making, constituting what we call an **IT Maturity Model**. For years, CEOs and HR directors have complained about the difficulty in finding people who can think in terms of both business and IT. It has been rare in the past to find these skills in the same employee, often assumed to be a quality of differing personality types. However, combining these two skills or modes of thought is becoming less and less of a luxury and more and more of a necessity to stay ahead of the game in organizational IT.

With the ascendancy of mobile, cloud computing, and their dynamic interaction with social media and information flow (what Gartner analysts refer to collectively as the "Nexus of Forces"), IT is becoming increasingly complex. But there are two key principles that supersede at all times, two main categories into which all other information must be fitted and integrated into a comprehensive IT Maturity Model. These involve advancing the *IT goals* on the one hand, whether through R&D, solution development, efficiency planning, or moving to the cloud, and advancing the organization's *financial goals* on the other. With their feet firmly planted in tech-land, with their heads in the cloud, with their face buried in an issue of Wired, or eyes glued to the latest tablet, this second piece has proven to be the more difficult for many IT directors.

As the landscape changes, and the tech world hops on the latest bandwagon, whether private cloud, hybrid cloud, PaaS, SaaS, XaaS, or the Internet of Things, it is incumbent on the IT director got to keep something else in mind: what your CEO or organizational head wants most, and how you can deliver that. Sometimes this will mean subordinating your own interests for a time, but developing a deep understanding of your CEOs main goals for the business, however explicitly or implicitly these have been communicated, is key for the IT Maturity Model. A word about CEOs here. Business owners, especially entrepreneurial ones, the kind you find in the SMB market, tend to be goal-oriented people, caring little for consistency, nomenclature, comprehensive or granular understanding of how things work. They see the pieces moving from 30000 feet, and see what has to happen next. They are forward thinking. They don't always see what you see in terms of organizational needs. It's important for you not to be perceived as someone who's either slowing down or, worse, derailing the train. Most likely they are also juggling far more than the organizational technology, and your request for the latest and greatest can seem like a resource drain after they've just met the HR Director, CFO, and the Account Manager.

Sometimes, the roles are reversed, and it is the CEO himself who wants to move forward with the latest tech development, convinced it can get their business to the next level, while the IT manager, more aware of some off the security concerns, who wants to put the brakes on. But really, we've got to embrace the change or risk becoming redundant, perceived as an obstacle to growth. We've certainly got to help our IT develop and remain cutting edge, but we also need to understand the impact that development has, not only on security, but on our organization's financial health.

Those two keys, managing IT development and achieving financial goals, have become essential parts of the IT manager's role more than ever before. Both are essential components of today's IT Maturity Model. In the chapters that follow, we'd like to explore some of these ongoing changes in detail and how they affect your role as an IT manager. It's exciting, it's evolving, it's dynamic. But make sure you keep the bigger picture in mind at all times. That's Mature IT!

Chapter 2

Users, Printer Problems, and BYOD

For techies, it's an exciting time. Some of what we've been foreseeing for years is finally coming to fruition. The true potential of the internet is being unleashed in radical new ways. Smart phones, smart business, smart cities. Whether inspired as kids through a science teacher, a parent, or watching Star Trek reruns, techies often deeply believe that advancing technology can provide a means of advancing society. At the very least, society's vast technology needs can help advance our financial goals, but shouldn't there be something more? Certainly this can be the case in the realm of cloud computing and its relationship to the Internet of Things, say, on a broad scale. IT people tend to like organization and efficiency, and like to envision a society that is implementing sweeping changes to that effect.

But even closer to home, most IT managers understand the benefit of cloud adoption for their organization. Scale up. Scale down. Monitor usage. Assign roles. Remove users. Onboarding. Training. System management. Security management. All this managed from a central location. This is music to the ear of the overworked, overextended IT director. Most would love to sink their grubby hands into the developing software to learning new skills and to wrap their head around new systems. This is what gets IT people fired up. Figuring out new tools, applying them, and demonstrating value, both of the new technology and of their exclusive expertise (vanity of vanities!).

Then, instead, they come into work, and the computer won't print. The ad exec needs his password reassigned in Active Directory once again. People can't get on the network with their laptop, their smart phone, their toothbrush. You calmly explain the toothbrush isn't in the cloud…yet. This layer of immediate need prevents you from getting to the more pressing system management issues: environment documentation, process improvement, policy creation, let alone researching new tech solutions.

At the enterprise level, and even in some SMBs this is compounded by travel and multi-locality. End user functionality issues are even more intricate, widespread, and complex in today's world. Right after resetting the ad exec's password and fixing the Jr. Accountant's printer, there's an executive sales call from Hong Kong, but they can't quite connect, and they need your help. The Nexus of Forces and cross-device integration means IT has to support increasing layers of complexity across the board, while at the same time supporting and improving efficiencies in IT for the organization.

Some IT departments do their best to address these issues with the following activity: a **Critical Areas of Need (CAN) assessment**. They begin by listing each area of need in their department, realizing that end user issues may be a "resource drain" during any given activity. But first, they establish the baseline by listing each area of need: *documentation, policy development, R&D,*

training, study, failover testing, process improvement. After the brainstorm session, rank them in order of importance. Then, for a given month, each area or domain is given a number of hours to realistically address the department needs in that area. This can be broken down on a chart, and be used to demonstrate both value and need to the C-level execs. You can show where the shortfalls and needs are. Do you need an assistant? What would the dollar value be? Will it scale? Performing a short "critical area of need" allocation can help clarify that picture and also graphically demonstrate where your stressors are, rather than leaving you in emotional reactive mode. It is much like establishing a monthly budget with your personal money. Instead of running out the final week of the month, you can determine where you're overspending, or how much more money you'll need to earn to support your lifestyle. It's important to perform this step with as many department members as possible to make sure everyone is on the same page, and understands how the department's time pie chart is carved up at a given time.

Critical Areas of Need (CAN) Assessment Completed (Figure 1.1)

Rank	Issue	Hours
1	Policies and Procedures	4
2	Workflows	4
3	Training	3
4	Documentation audit	2
5	Failover/security testing	1
6	R&D	2
7	New Solution Assessment	2

Bring Your Own Device

This short organizational exercise can help plug some holes, keep you moving, help get breathing room from the CFO, but it won't account for the shift in another area of IT: devices. There used to be much tighter control on organizational integrity. IT managers might worry about end users catching viruses by surfing on the wrong websites, about system crashes, and the like. But by and large, there were few points of interface with outside systems. We had onsite servers, closed systems with the same OS and cloned images on each device. Remember that? Instead, today we've got Windows, Mac, Android, tablets, laptops, desktops, smart phones, Chromebooks, Hoppers, uppers, downers, screamers, laughers. Some employees bring their own device; one is finicky about Macs, the other about Windows. There is, at the very least, a lot more to worry about from the point of view of security.

Security threats, Trojans, malware, none of this is new. What is new are platform agnostic threats, targeting multiple OSs. Ideally, we would provide simultaneous updates, patches, and security deployments across the board, ensuring robust, widespread security. Now? Developers aren't necessarily providing patches at the same time. Staggering updates across multiple devices and operating systems in a large environment means vulnerability. Monitoring data going in and out of these environments is next to impossible. You provide general policies and guidelines and cross your fingers, hoping employees abide by them across the board. Sensitive data is at risk. How many times have you heard or read about the stolen laptop containing client information, passwords, or medical information costing thousands in damage control?

Yes, security is an issue. Data sprawl is an issue. But the old command and control stance won't cut it anymore, either. Deep breaths. All is not lost. It's going to be okay.

Chapter 3

Control, Now You Have It, Now You Don't

The first step toward IT Maturity, as we mention above, is the ability to think in terms of both improving technology and advancing business goals. But before we address that combination, let's take a look at some of the current difficulties inherent in the role of the IT manager. As your organization's IT guru, you're the gatekeeper, the guardian, the goalie. Only you don't have nearly the same amount of control anymore, because of the spread of data across platforms and devices. What's a security minded IT director to do? This organizational porousness can cause many IT managers to respond with a command and control mindset. Many organizations we've consulted with have reached a point of impasse here. They have a longtime IT director who has become suspicious, insular, and avoidant. In his mind, the system doesn't have the integrity he's used to. He's already in a state of stress simply with the organizational infrastructure. To him, the network infrastructure is a house of cards and he can no longer keep the door shut. The slightest gust of wind from outside could bring the whole thing tumbling down. To the executives, however, who would like to move forward with meetings, projects, offerings, services, in short, expand their business, running into a buzz saw in their IT director time after time has become frustrating. Some have taken the drastic measure of firing them, other times it's the IT directors themselves who leave out of frustration.

We hear frustrated executives saying "they've simply become a 'No' person!" And indeed they seem threatened by any new initiative, recommendation, or offering, feeling it might fragment an already overstressed system. In cloud computing terms, you always want to have 20% compute and storage capacity overage for sudden spikes in usage or data. In the mind of the IT director, however, the operation is already at 95% per cent capacity or higher. They becomes like Scotty, saying she's giving all she's got. And still things threaten to break apart. This can create a divisive, unproductive culture. What we advise the executives is that this is a stressful, transitional time in IT. As things change rapidly, IT directors often have their hands full with managing their system and don't have the leisure to train and keep up with changes, let alone implement best practices in that regard.

 But the IT manager does have to change. No, not the plaid Kirkland brand shirt with the pocket protector. That's a given. Engineers have an image to uphold, after all. But they do have to change their mentality. **IT managers have to see their role as that of facilitator, as strategic policy developer within their organization**. They've got to think through problems old and new and provide best practice guidelines and policies to that effect. This is one of the changes required to maintain an up-to-date IT Maturity Model.

Today, a command and control mindset will simply keep an organization bogged down, unable to boost sales, greatly limiting profit and revenue, presumably one of the main reasons the business exists. When this happens, suspicions set in. Does the IT director understand what a business is for? Do they see it as one big toy box and don't want anyone else to play with their toys? CEOs start to take a sharp eye to the budget line items. What's this for R&D? What's that for training? Please tell the members of the jury where you were on the night of November 15th, exactly, when this completely unnecessary router was purchased! Not feeling the IT director is actively trying to help build the business, they begin to be seen as an obstruction at best, and at worst (wait for it…) a mooch! This isn't just because the office donut box is mysteriously empty every time they've passed by.

What will likely happen is either the obstructive-protective mindset will lead to the IT director's replacement or the company losing market position given the lack of agility and the loss of competitive advantage. Essentially, trying to meet business objectives in an environment moving at light speed with standard command and control mindset no longer works, partly due to mobile devices, multiple operating systems, and the advent of private and public clouds. The cat is already out of the bag. Your organization's IT is already outside the walls of the office everywhere you look. The ad exec takes the laptop to a coffee shop on Tuesday mornings. The CEO works from home on Friday. One has a Mac, the other a PC (who are you to judge?).

The state of the current IT director is much like that of the nervous parent whose child is headed off to college. You provide guidelines, you raise them right. You give the occasional talk. You let them come home one weekend a month to do the laundry, but you can't make sure they're in bed before 2 AM the night before a final. Only, whereas in real life, the likelihood is high that the child will move back in for a while after college, in IT, it ain't happening. They're gone and they ain't coming back. Employees in your organization are conversing, exchanging, and interacting on multiple platforms, with multiple devices in multiple locations, at work, at home, *and* in public. But uptime, data security, and performance is naturally still a concern. Not only do the employees need to be able to get information, stay productive, and connect with each other, but important meetings need to run smoothly with clients as well. And just like your organization, the companies you connect with are experiencing the same kind of cross-device, multi-platform usage.

 Let's take a look at some elements a **robust security policy** might include to mitigate risk in this crazy world of employee, device, and data sprawl. You may also like to include a summary of possible risks for each implementation in the policy for full transparency, if only to alleviate your own nagging concerns, and to show that you've thought the problem through to a high degree. Some kind of centralized console or *remote management software* (RMS) will help policy management across several end points and layers. Proactive threat intelligence technology is almost a necessity at the enterprise layer. You want to make sure you've got the latest and greatest inspecting your system looking out for those ever developing threats. Then, you want to make sure data going in and out of company gateways and endpoints stays encrypted. And, call me crazy, but deploying a virtualized environment seems like an intuitive way to keep personal and professional device management split. Beyond that, it can even mitigate patching, update, and security implementation concerns across multiple operating systems. Shuffling past me in the coffee shop the other day, an upbeat stranger asked me how I got the Windows OS on what was clearly a Macbook Pro. The lesson here: virtualization won't just help your organization with security and ultimately profit margins, it will also impress strangers in coffee shops wielding impressively large espresso based beverages!

To summarize, adopting a dual mindset of thinking in terms of tech solutions and business solutions is the starting point; this is the first step toward what we're calling an IT

Maturity Model. The next step is to consider practical solutions to some of the pressing problems at this particular point of transition in IT that allow you to become a facilitator rather than an obstacle to organizational progress, including remote management, threat detection, encryption, and possibly virtualized environments. Now that we've touched on this briefly here, let's take a closer look at some of these issues, including the kooky world of backup and data recovery (oy gevalt!).

Chapter 4

Backups: Why Can't They Ever Get This $#!T To Work?

No, seriously. Why doesn't it work? Like ever. No, really. It never works. This seems like such an age old problem, it's as if written in tablets of stone in ancient hieroglyphics. We can imagine an Egyptian wall, a human body draped in cloth with a bird's head and a finger pointing to the ancient symbol for "desktop" sinking in lines of water, next to a boat with a lightning bolt running through it. Rescue, confounded. It seems like a time-worn adage, set down by Benjamin Franklin in his *Poor Richard's Almanac*: "Though in the darkness danger mayhap lurks/the disaster recovery system never friggin' works."

The new realities of IT affect this area, too. The complexity of infrastructure, system, device, and application dynamics require newer, more innovative approaches to backup and disaster recovery as well. Just like maintaining the same mentality of command and control in the IT environment can bog down your company, applying the same set of solutions for BDR can be fatal for an IT infrastructure. New problems call for new solutions.

To that end, let's take a look at some different backup methodologies that could be of benefit. You want to demonstrate your expertise in this area to alleviate the fears of executives and company decision makers, or any stakeholder for that matter, should questions or issues arise, right? Thought so. Though the IT director often walks around cutting a wide swath, sneering at the idiots in his way who dive for cover in the blinding light of his brilliance, beneath the surface there is often a veritable storm of insecurity, often in some proportion to the lack of system integrity he perceives. Sometimes this leads to a crack in the façade, a blow up at the boss, who doesn't get it, a "how the hell should I know?!?" to the sales rep who wants to know where her spreadsheet went. IT directors have been known to lock the office door, just to have a good cry. So let's shore up your backup knowledge here. Add to the tools in the old tool belt. You'll get your swagger back in no time!

 Obviously, a good **disaster recovery plan** starts with establishing *recovery time objectives* (RTOs) and *recovery point objectives* (RPOs). In both cases, you're basically establishing the highest acceptable amount of downtime and the highest allowable amount of data loss between recovery points. As these go down, of course, cost tends to go up (see that? business hat on!) One way to go is to componentize the backup system into smaller pieces based on function. Make sense? This means breaking up the data protection according to where the data resides. In practical terms, this could mean breaking recovery operations into separate tiers, like *content recovery*, *data operations*, and *full system* backup and recovery measures, complete with full redundancy, load balancing, and elimination of any single points of failure.

It could also mean getting more granular and componentizing your sub-systems. Depending on your infrastructure, maybe you'll have to think of front-end and back-end blocks as distinct components and subdivide further. Within those subgroups of front-end and back-end, say, you may need to break down further, running, for example, load-balanced IIS servers in concert with a pair of servers running application roles (is my SharePoint side showing?). However complex the setup or however many components you establish, you then ensure a layer of backup and recovery for that specific layer with increasing degrees of complexity involved.

Cold failover is the traditional mode of waiting until a low usage point, usually in the middle of the night, shutting off access to the system and performing a wholesale backup. This might make sense for some smaller organizations or systems where most access is onsite for a clearly delimited amount of time. But for many organizations, spread across time zones, or even multiple continents, this won't work very well, or only on rare, predetermined occasions.

Another option is the *warm failover*. This involves data copied on multiple servers simultaneously with a standby system available. Should the system fail, or a user get kicked out for one reason or another, they can log back on, since the data was copied to another server available in standby mode. This is a more complicated and more expensive model, but for many organizations, the loss of productivity and data would be much higher with a cold recovery.

Another option is to run a *hot backup* (I'm picking up on some kind of temperature analogy, here). This involves backing up systems when they are active and available to users. For complex systems, this presents a much better option than the cold backup, performed only when the system is unused and unavailable. This means, with a hot backup, no downtime is required to back up the system. This carries some risks, such as inconsistency with the data at point of backup (always a risk at this level), and possible performance loss while the backup is being performed. It can be expensive, so the IT manager needs to weigh options and find the right price point that mitigates risk sufficiently.

The advent of cloud computing is a possible windfall in this area. One of its major selling points is robust failover and BDR capabilities. Within the cloud computing environment, different hybrid and private cloud combinations exist to reduce single points of failure at every layer. For most businesses, private cloud options with multiple data centers, comprehensive redundancy measures, and backup recovery solutions in place will more than do the trick. Other companies may have media rich applications or data in use, or federal guidelines in place that require some amount of data to be stored onsite. Backing up to cloud locations with multiple replications a day via a hybrid cloud option provides security and flexibility to allow our IT director to unlock the door, wipe away his tears, and strut back around with his usual sneer of cold command, like a Sith Lord on the command center looking down at his hapless, trembling officers. Side note: is it possible Darth didn't have time to read his Christmas copy of "Carrots and Sticks Don't Work" to shape his management style? Food for thought.

In keeping with our goal of business mindedness along with the IT director's vast technical expertise, it would be helpful to establish short-hand price points for each options with a note on the value and relevance for your organization. Present the option to the C level executives along with your recommendation and reasoning. Show you've got the best interest of the P&L spreadsheet (that's profit & loss, if you're really green on the business side) in mind with your decision making. That way, the Cs will feel like you're on their side. So get out there and turn that "No" into a "Here are some things we could do!" Don't forget, people who like to feel important also like to make decisions every now and then. Maybe even present your options on official company letterhead, or try the PowerPoint template with the company logo. Or list the five options with the company mascot next to your recommended option. These people didn't spend three days at a catered seminar developing the company color scheme for nothing. Remember, the scratched back scratches back!

While the IT Maturity Model combines developing technology in concert with business goals, we can't neglect the basic aspects of developing IT either. Increasing complexity in IT calls for innovative security solutions as well. The security game in IT is always going to be a back and forth, a tug of war between the hackers with their security threats and organizations with their security solutions. Keeping on top of changes in this area is no small feat. In our next chapter we'll examine security issues beyond backup and data recovery in some depth.

Chapter 5

Security – It's an Inside Job!

It's Hard Out Here for an IT Director

As we've established, maintaining the security of your network is now ten times more complex. First off, you've got security risks from internal employees. If your company has any amount of frequent turnover, with employee loyalty not building up over time, this can be even scarier. Employees carry sensitive data across devices, with a special increase in mobile use. This means they're transacting and exchanging information on smart phones, personal laptops, storing data on personal email, in public clouds, sending confidential info on public networks, and of course, with those hi def camera doohickies on every device imaginable, your data just might be securely stored on someone else's private network as well.

"OK," you say, "I get it. Things are dangerous for network and data security," you say. "But I also remember from my college communications course that presenting problems without discussing solutions breeds only cynical worldviews. For shame!" I'm glad you brought that up, actually. Beyond the macro level touched on way back in chapter 4, we'd like to take a look at some different security methodologies that help mitigate some of the top risks we're seeing across the board.

Let's conduct a little thought experiment: take a random employee's phone and ask yourself, "if this device were stolen or lost, how safe would company data be?" For some companies, who have no policy in place, this could mean disaster. Take the same device running an app on a public wifi, which could introduce malware into the system. Many end users have so many devices that they lose track of where they store data. They may move from desktop to smart phone to tablet to laptop throughout the course of a day, now on the local system, now on the company virtual machine, now on the public cloud through a local MS OneDrive or Google drive. There's simply no way to curtail this aspect of current usage. That's not to say there's nothing to be done, of course.

First and foremost, you need strong, comprehensive and clearly communicated policies and procedures in place. I'm going to take a slight detour here and talk about the communication piece. Several companies we've worked with have a policy in place, written black on white in the employee handbook, but never communicated in plain English in an all company forum where employees actually encounter, hear, and internalize the information with a chance to process it, and ask questions, raise concerns, provide feedback, signal buy in, and so on. Making sure you set aside time at an all company meeting, whether quarterly or monthly, this information has to be passed along to all. Even an all staff email with this particular policy as an attachment and key points highlighted is a step in the right direction. But all the research, discussion, decision making, and time writing up policy is wasted if no one knows about it. Heck, even if you steal the policy from a consulting company or cut and paste it from somewhere and mischievously set it to company letterhead, the word must get out. Rant over. Back to the main point of the chapter.

The robust security policy should determine whether you will allow company applications to run alongside private applications on any given device, for example. Although it's obviously best practice to keep these separate, that's not always feasible. This could be further subdivided by company role and application type. Your policy should determine who has access to what sections of the company infrastructure. The factors of productivity and security have to be balanced sensibly here, of course, with a company wide **Access Map**. This involves mapping out the different sections of the company network (as suggested by the above title "Access Map"), like internal IT information governing networking, infrastructure, passwords, active directory, etc. in one category. Then list web site, social media, and customer facing applications in another. Third, put down documentation and data management applications in yet another category. Finally, assign in detail or by department who has access to which areas, and at what level. This could be included in employee handbook and included at an all company meeting and reinforced during new employee onboarding.

Simple Access Map (Figure 1.2)

Internal IT	Customer Facing	Data Management:
Networking, Infrastructure, AD, Passwords	Web Site, Social Media Applications, Passwords	Internal Documentation, Client Documentation, Workflow, Email
IT Department Executives Department Managers	Executives Marketing Director Communications Manager Social Media Coordinator IT Department	Executives Department Manager IT Department All Staff (read only)

Another best practice is for each employee to live out of their virtual machine provided by the company. These can be spun up with any and all important mission critical applications and data needed, and are customizable per user. If the computer battery dies, or if the wifi goes out at the coffee shop, or if the kid spills his milk on the keyboard, the virtual machine will stay exactly as it was at last point of login. Behold the genius of the internet! Currently, these aren't always smoothly integrated with mobile devices, though that will likely change soon. This provides a ton of advantages, with security, encryption, application, remote management capabilities, and so on. If only it were that simple all the time. Beyond the individual end user, most businesses have other aspects of security to consider, like sending data to partners, client access, and working on public wifi.

In addition to having the robust policies in place and communicated, there are several strategies to consider implementing to help maximize security for the network. One such strategy is a *remote connectivity* option. This typically involves an application provided by your managed service provider or at least a vendor that provides enterprise level applications for remote support, like GoTo Meeting, Team Viewer or Webex. Unless this is rolled into your fixed support fee, there's usually a fee from the vendor for providing business level services here, though you'll likely have the option to try out different applications as "test drive" scenarios, provided by the vendor's sales team. Again, with our business hat on, connecting with a sales rep may allow you to negotiate a better price than the one listed on the company web site. Those sales reps want their commission, after all.

Another element to consider is *email encryption*. Usually, while your connection to public email options like Gmail is encrypted, the messages you send are not, nor are the messages in their stored state. You also can't be sure the connection on the recipient end or at several other points of connection are secure (heard of the NSA's PRISM program?).

Sometimes applied across the board, and sometimes used as a plug-in, encrypted email can be applied to your internal communication more easily. Sometimes it can cause problems when sending encrypted messages to users outside the network who don't have the same encryption software. Two possible downsides of encryption are that header information is not encrypted, and encryption makes folder searches difficult for quick information. Short of encryption, one best practices is to cut up sensitive information into several chunks and send separately, changing the heading, making is slightly more difficult for hacked information to be pieced together and misused.

Yet another element to consider in the policy is social media communication guidelines. What information is appropriate to provide? What is off limits? Social media marketing provides a powerful opportunity for companies to raise brand awareness, increase profile, target a specific audience with a brand appropriate message, and allow customers and partners a peek behind the curtain. All these are positive elements. And usually social media policies govern practical issues, like what can get an employee in trouble. Is it poking fun at the boss publicly? Is it describing a product that's still in development? Is it congratulating a new hire who may have expert level skill set coveted by competitors? For our purposes here, that is security, identifying what information is appropriate to communicate publicly has to include defining precisely what constitutes sensitive data and how to handle it.

Hopefully your network, system, and data stay secure at all times. Obviously, this requires a proactive approach of monitoring, maintenance, and staying up to date on patching. Security is an inside job because as much as outside hackers make news at this or that corporation every now and then, more often than not it's lack of proper policies, procedures, and internal systems that cause security issues. Taking a proactive approach to security is an essential component of the Mature IT model. This seems obvious to the IT professional, but keeping the business piece in mind, security concerns have to be weighed against productivity and budgetary concerns to help achieve business goals for your organization. Let's not, shall we, forget that part.

Chapter 6

Process Sucks (But It's Still Necessary)

Dig if you will the immortal words of that luminous artist from a bygone era, Mr. Vanilla Ice. *If you got a problem, yo, I'll solve it/ Check out the hook while the DJ revolves it!* Musical artistry aside, Mr. Ice represents your average IT manager in that he's mainly a problem solver (or so he would have us think!). Now the problems can range from small scale to large scale, micro to macro, SMB to enterprise and back again. But what we see time and again in companies we consult with are *reactive* postures. When this very mindset of problem solving predominates, and there is lack of attention to systems and processes to assess system health, efficiency, to address service needs, to align practices, to synchronize data sets, and well, let's just say that cracks form.

There are a few key points at which these chinks in the armor tend to develop. One huge area of concern for many IT departments is lack of proper **documentation**. I know, I know. Shoot me now, you say. But let's hold off on the trigger there for a moment. One reason, often an unconscious one, why IT directors don't implement proper documentation guidelines is out of a fear of being redundant. If I document accurately what's going on in the organization, so the thinking goes, then it's no longer in my head exclusively, and anyone can step in and do the job. I'm no longer absolutely necessary. See the command and control logic at work? It's fear driven thinking and ultimately hurts the company. The only way to maximize efficiency of your department is not only to establish proper documentation for the network, systems, changes, patches, upgrades, and so on, but to hold department members accountable for maintaining the same level of documentation. That documentation will provide covering in case something does go wrong, providing proof that you held up your end, and it was system, hardware, software, or vendor error, not yours. And even if it was your department's error, following the documentation can provide the quickest way to finding the error and eliminating it. Establishing strong, granular level documentation policies are key.

This can be simplified of course with internal ticketing systems, should you have need on that level. Getting everyone on board with a ticketing system to automate some of these processes can be a huge help. Here you can standardize processes, ensure smooth hand-off, ideally with integration into your email system. Request capturing, work logging, time capturing, documentation, and project collaboration can all be managed from a central console, with dashboards for capturing how quickly given projects are closed, how many of a given project type is requested, where the most time is spent, needed parts, vendor information, etc. Depending on your organization and department size, such processes have become essential to efficiency and effectiveness.

Another area where we see lack of adequate documentation is in the area of diagrams. Data flow diagrams, for example, help chart the circulation of information within your network infrastructure and organization. Often, the IT director or manager has this in their head and can drill down with a bit of concentration, but making this available and accessible for the department is essential for simple project hand off and maintaining internal efficiency. This requires having a comprehensive understanding of departments, roles, and associated technology by department and position. This is also a huge help if the ticketing system you use needs further refinement and customization beyond out of the box features. We often see these two pieces poorly coordinated. There may be data flow diagrams and a ticketing system, but one isn't driving the other and project hand-off fails to go smoothly.

Cracks develop in internal processing, pretty soon the sales rep is giving the field tech the stink eye in the break room, and before you know it there's an outside consulting agency at $3500 a pop in to conduct team building workshops and organized group hugs. You can stop the madness single handedly by having diagrams in place and informing solutions and applications you implement to help accomplish your work.

In any organization clear roles and clear expectations for those roles are a key point of productivity, job satisfaction, and organizational success. Getting departmental workflows together falls under the same umbrella of accurate documentation. In reactive mode, we accomplish work ad hoc, which can cause the occasional dropped ball, project slow down, or downright failure. At the very least ambiguity creates anxiety and frustration, which affects the organizational culture. With the workflows in place, you can update them as needed, and ramp up new employees far more quickly. Beyond the flow within your own department, this can provide a touchstone, an example, a baseline for the organization as a whole, who let's face it, is probably less apt to think it terms of organizational structure and information flow than the seasoned and chiseled veterans of the IT department. Setting the tone for organizational efficiency can provide a backbone for information flow in other areas of your organization. You help shape to a great degree how data flows between different business units.

If you're like most IT professionals, all this organizational brouhaha probably has you reaching for the remote, your sandwich, or clicking through your email. To many it can seem like getting bogged down in unnecessary details. That's precisely the thinking we're trying to protect against here. Adopting an IT Maturity Model means precisely getting into the nitty-gritty of your organizational dynamics, understanding how all the pieces fit, how the entire sales and project lifecycle moves from start to finish. This moves you from a glorified mechanic to a business asset. Until you make this shift, it's often hard to justify moving into next gen technology and migrating into the cloud, advocating increased efficient methodology like that offered by cloud-based offerings. You've got to demonstrate why this is valuable, and how it can increase efficiency. Any executive worth their salt is going to want to see some kind of projected ROI before signing off on larger cloud projects with upfront costs. Security can be a selling point, but that alone isn't the bread and butter. We'll outline a more comprehensive picture of an IT Maturity Model below that can provide common language and framework. But for now, let us stress the importance of understanding what your organization is doing in detail at the process level. This moves you from reactive to proactive mode, allowing you to anticipate needs, and propose solutions before problems occur. For some executives used to more traditional IT, this would be like the mechanic coming to the house, and letting them know they need to trade in because the alternator is going to blow out in two or three months, and not only that, the mechanic has already researched the best trade in deal with the top three options for their next vehicle, tailored to their family's precise needs. Understanding what the company needs at different levels allows you to do just that for the organization. Getting process and procedures ironed out allow you to be proactive, and then you can get your grubby mitts on the latest and greatest, because you've demonstrated why it's going to help. And speaking of the latest and greatest, with all the cloud talk you hear these days, we'll take a look at different cloud models in the next chapter and how they can help organizations. So bring your galoshes and let's go for a brief tour of cloudkookooland.

Chapter 7

Cumulous, Nebulous, and Other Clouds

Before you get your cloud on, you want to show you know how to make it rain (yes, we coined that one!). At least that's what we've been trying to establish so far. This concept of an IT Maturity Model we've been driving home here is about a comprehensive approach. Enterprise level businesses are adopting cloud computing at a record pace, but really it's the SMB market where cloud computing can provide an edge. Where we've seen the cloud be a windfall for IT directors is in agility, scalability, and efficiency. But we'll get to that.

Cloud computing is still tricky for some people to wrap their heads around. Already skittish about tech talk, the metaphor of the cloud to describe computing makes them short-circuit. And it really is a bit misleading. It makes it sound like Ray Kurzweil's futurism has already come to pass. Tiny nano-servers hovering overhead, ready to store and channel data to anywhere, anytime. It all sounds rather spooky. This means you'll need simple ways of describing it whether to rank and file employees or to decision makers.

A simple way to talk about cloud to your stakeholders is in terms of utility computing. That often does the trick, since most people have a framework for that, but still find themselves a bit hazy on all this cloud talk. About 120 years ago, businesses had to create electricity onsite. Now, we tap into a grid, which keeps cost low, since we all make use of it. Same thing with cloud computing. The servers are offsite, the compute and storage is prepaid, often on a per user basis. Voila. Utility model. The problem with this simple explanation is there are other terms out there in the ether already (pun intended). People have at least of heard of private cloud, public cloud, and hybrid cloud. The problem here is most people in our day and age are visual processors. That means when you say a phrase, for most people, an image pops in their head. Cloud? Easy enough. Cumulus. Cirrus. Nebulous. We all remember laying on the grass as a kid and imagining a castle or a dragon floating past. Dark clouds rolling in means rain's a-coming. But private cloud? Or worse. Hybrid cloud?

Recently, I was at a conference buying a souvenir for my son and got into a conversation with the shop's cashier, who also happened to be the owner. Eventually she got around to asking "what do you do?" Used to business conversations, I rattled off "I run an IT solutions and consulting company." Almost as an aside, I added "We place a lot of focus on fleshing on cloud computing services, too." That ended the warm, friendly conversation pretty abruptly. The shop owner basically rolled her eyes, saying "sure, fella, whatever that means."

These can be the kinds of obstacles we face in conversation with people, sometimes even within our organizations. The experience provided a stark contrast to the facile tech speak at the conference. There's an assumed subset of knowledge and an inside jargon we can get caught up in. We assume everyone's roughly on the same page. This can be worse if you work in a tech hub like Silicon Valley or Austin or

Seattle. It doesn't help that we use ambiguous terms and lack standardized definitions within the industry. One example is different implied definitions of hybrid cloud.

Let's be clear. This is not a book about cloud computing. But this *is* a book about an IT Maturity Model. And right now as well as for the foreseeable future, cloud computing is going to be a part of the conversation of a robust, mature IT strategy. With that in mind, let's get into a description of current cloud computing models and how they can benefit businesses. One key to keep in mind is simply the core idea behind cloud computing in the first place: location. Where is your data stored?

Privacy, Please

OK. Since you're in IT, we'll assume you have some knowledge of the private cloud computing option. But we'll give a simple refresher before getting to some of the specific benefits of private cloud computing and how to integrate it into a Maturity Model. If you've been in IT for any amount of time, you will know the traditional legacy hardware model of an organizational network. You've got the central server in some storage space, with fans whirring to keep the thing cool. A few racks, some flashing lights. A bunch of cords. Sound familiar? For some, it's still reality, so let's not call it archaic just yet.

Going with a private cloud means moving whatever data you had on that server to an offsite server. "Pure" private cloud means this server in the data center is exclusively allocated to your organization. To be able to do set up a data center, cloud providers have to make sure the place is secure, cool, dry, flood, fire, and earthquake proof. Secure usually means the center is guarded with key card access only. OK, that's the physical security. But the real security benefit is the redundant nature of cloud computing. To be able to sell cloud computing space widely, providers have to make it properly secure. This involves system redundancy at every layer with failover solutions in place. If there's a problem on one server, or some kind of outage (mostly caused by updates and new implementations, ironically), security software will cause your company's data, which is periodically copied to a second server, to cue up on the backup server. In the past, a server outage means you're basically screwed. Now, with failover and load balancing by experts who manage these issues, all the time, you're covered.

Beyond security, the first obvious savings here is on the hardware itself. As you're aware, every new tech refresh cycle can run about 30K for a small to midsize business. That's a huge expense every few years that the executive, and whoever else manages the budget, would love to get rid of, or use to, say, stock the break room with a higher grade of coffee. An obvious second cost is physical maintenance and insurance, but these costs are obviously much lower. Another gain is in the area of software maintenance, patching, upgrades, and software licensing. If your IT department is understaffed (is there any other kind these days?), you know this can be a huge time drain for yourself and your staff, at least periodically.

Given the nature of many organizations, two other immediate benefits are gained by moving to offsite servers. When it comes to buying a business level server, you don't have a ton of options. You might be stuck buying a server that's twice the size of your actual needs every refresh cycle. Moving to a rack on an offsite server means you buy what you need. If you have a sudden project that requires doubling workforce size in the short-term (not unheard of for small businesses in a collaborative sphere), this might overload traditional servers, whereas in cloud computing, you can spin up more VMs, and pay for that usage for the duration of need only. This is what scalability and efficiency refer to, terms often lost in the marketing nebula. On the application layer, you usually have some kind of dashboard that shows usage rates, peak times, mission critical applications, unused applications, computing speed, and so on. You can now make data driven decisions on your IT spend. If it's so simple and so beneficial, why doesn't everyone do it? Well, usually, there are upfront migration costs, first of all. This is usually less than buying a new server, but even at comparable costs, you know it's the last one you'll ever have to buy. Also, many providers run on a business model that allows you to roll in migration costs into monthly support costs over time, reducing upfront expenses by quite a bit. Side note: rolling upfront costs into later payments is called "amortizing." If you want to fast track at least the perception that you're keeping up with the business end of things, start using that word in meetings when the new product offering comes up. "Hey, I'm just wondering, can we *amortize* that?" Instant brownie points!

Another issue can be local bandwidth. This is part of any initial discussion or Cloud Readiness Assessment. Basically, if it ain't there, it ain't there. There can be options with the telecom provider, but with low bandwidth, it can be a choppy road ahead. If the offsite data center is the heart of your infrastructure, low bandwidth is the clogged artery. For cloud service providers who take on clients with low bandwidth, the headaches are many. All the end user knows is their service isn't there, and they want someone to scream at, especially if the field is high pressure enough, like, say, healthcare. One positive note here is that telecom companies are fighting to keep up with market demands and bandwidth levels should increase across the board. In the short term, that's not a cure all for everyone. In the early stages of cloud adoption, this was more of a problem than today. A quick google search on "telecom bandwidth problem" and "cloud computing" shows articles on this topic, but tellingly, many are from several years before cloud computing hit the mainstream.

Going Public

OK, private cloud computing provides some benefits to organizations. I get it. But what's the difference between private and public cloud? In many people's minds, a cloud is a cloud is a cloud (which is technically true). But let's split the hairs here. With private cloud, you've got a dedicated network environment offsite. This dedicated space and the security measures can be necessary for industry compliance issues. Private cloud environments are pretty much designed to meet Sarbanes Oxley, PCI, and HIPAA compliance requirements, for example, if that's your bag.

But when does a public cloud make sense, you ask? Hold your horses, now. First let's take a look at what private and public clouds have in common: both provide scalability, instant provisioning, virtualized resources, and the ability to expand the server base quickly. The key difference is simply this: with public cloud, you're data is on a server rack along with several other clients. This is the truest form of computing as a utility. But even here, the definitions get tricky. With ever developing technology, some of the virtual separation available means for all intents and purposes, your data is safe, secure, and private. The line between public and private cloud is certainly beginning to blur.

The security issue can be a little trickier here, though. Since you're sharing the space, the public cloud option doesn't allow for the same high level security requirements that some industries mandate. It's a better (and cheaper!) option for high use applications that experience heavy spikes in usage or "incremental use," collaborative projects involving non-critical data, possibly Software as a Service (SaaS) from a vendor with proven security measures in place. The danger is simply that someone who knows what they're doing can endanger the integrity of your system and compromise your data. Beyond intentional security risk, there is also human error. Unintended mismanagement could open your data to other users potentially, given the multi-tenancy architecture.

Other huge considerations in public cloud space are related to ownership and exploits. The ownership question seems a bit strange, but true: some public cloud providers have fine print in the contract that identifies them as the owner of data in their cloud. This is to provide additional coverage for them for any possible legal processes in possible data loss. The exploits issue is complicated by virtualization, given the extra points of connection (server host, guest to guest, host to guest, and guest to host). That said, public cloud options are still more secure in many instances than on-premise network environments. Part of the reason is that massive companies have a huge stake in the success of cloud computing, and even at the SMB level, hosting and managed service providers have security experts who devote a large part off their time, training, certification, and daily work in managing security for cloud environments, whereas your onsite IT manager has to wear twenty different hats, much as they'd love to spend their weekends reading *Cloud Hosting Security for Dummies*. But we'll get to weekends in a later chapter.

According to cloud hosting gurus, the public cloud is gaining steam big time, as it continues to develop and become more secure. Part of this is the enterprise level offerings from AWS, Microsoft Azure, and Google. Gartner's analysis shows the bigger savings with similar agility and efficiency means the public cloud architectures and hybrid models will be huge going forward. However, private cloud options are the only option for some industries, given those strict data storage guidelines.

Many-Headed Hybrids

Usually, the term hybrid cloud refers to the combination of public cloud and onsite management in some fashion. This is one of the more attractive options for many companies, especially at the small to mid-size level. Given budget limitations, and also given application specific expertise to manage work in-house, some companies simply need to keep data onsite in some capacity. But these companies may also want to take advantage of, say, archiving options in the public cloud, which can provide exponentially more space. If you've lived in an apartment but also rented a local storage space for larger items like your kayak, scuba gear, water skis and Sherpa hat, you know exactly how this works. Just as you need to keep your loofa, tea kettle, and eye shade in the home for quick access, your company may need to keep its day to day mission critical application management onsite.

The hybrid cloud is often the most amenable to the IT director, who can feel their job security threatened by the ascent of cloud computing. Instead, the hybrid cloud model solidifies their position, as the primary point of contact with the hosting and managed service provider. The IT director can now focus on managing core service offerings and offload other elements to the services provider. This arrangement can be even more symbiotic, with contract verbiage included to allow for escalation of tough to handle projects that outstrip the IT director's expertise, or that require quicker turn around than he is equipped to handle.

Using the home analogy from above, if I have my fireplace crackling away at home to warm the hearth and ward off winter's chill, let's say a bit of discarded newspaper is left too close, catches fire, and begins to singe the carpet. I can grab a fire extinguisher while the rest of the family does the stop, drop, and roll. If at the same time, however, my friendly neighborhood arsonist sets fire to my rooftop, the upstairs bath, and the corner of my den, threatening the entirety of my extensive Garth Brooks CD collection, well, I'd do well to ring the fire brigade. And if the same people ran the fire brigade and offered the local storage space for my cache of seldom used rock climbing gear, then I've got a managed service provider that provides cloud hosting. Only, unlike those pesky cloud hosting and managed service providers, the fire-brigade-slash-storage-companies aren't constantly flooding my inbox with white paper offers, thank heavens.

Be that as it may, with a hybrid cloud model, you still need someone looking after configuration management, change control, and security. Hybrid cloud models vary widely, though. It's a broad enough term to cover combinations of onsite, public, and private cloud hosting options. The right configuration will be based on an individual scenario of your organization, depending on your specific configuration requirements. Data storage needs, work type requirements, automation, communication needs, application latency and performance needs, partners and compatibility, security guidelines, and business analytics are all part of the consideration. With your business hat on, consider the top five essential elements of your current configuration and to what extent they could be made more efficient, more secure, or more scalable with some form of cloud adoption.

The next step in moving toward an IT Maturity Model is to consider how these changes can become business drivers. In the SMB market, from a business perspective, the big three issues are managing cash, people, and risk. These concerns will naturally have different inflections at different organizations, depending on current goals and needs. Maybe you've got sales in the pipeline, but need to scale to perform the work. Maybe you've tapped out a small market and are looking to expand. At this point, company growth strategy, department efficiency, productivity, and simplifying processes, all can be part of the discussion. What the IT Maturity Model helps with is setting priorities. Like any department serving superordinate organizational goals, internal department goals can come into conflict with overall company goals.

Let's say you're experiencing updates and patching as a huge time suck and need help in that area with a junior tech hire. You happen to know your HR department is interviewing for a Jr. Account Manager and looking to add consulting and project management contractors to the payroll. Rather than throwing your hands up and saying "these idiots are gonna sink the ship," you can put the calculation together in dollars and cents. How much is it costing the company to have you perform this work for one hour? How much are they charging the client for the patching for an hour? What other work could you be doing at that time? Could it be billed at a higher rate? Could additional sales go through by freeing up your time? Can adding a cloud layer help coordinate and reduce response time, delivery time, or the entire operational lifecycle? These are typically management concerns, and many average IT pros just want to dive into the work, then end up getting frustrated. By adding the business dimension to your thinking you can construct persuasive arguments to get what you need to run your department. For any decision you'd like to see made, or any decision you'd like to challenge, showing its revenue implications is your best bet to getting it seen through. Maybe the problem in the department isn't one of stupid decisions, but ill-informed decisions. Maybe a more consistent communications loop could help shore up a lot of the gaps. How much more valuable your position would be if you were the one to initiate processes like that!

 Here's a quick exercise to assess your current status within your organization. Reflect on the quality of your input on decisions that affect your department. Are your requests and recommendations valued by upper management? Are you communicating the financial implications of your requests? Are you making the connection between IT solution and revenue? When you provide options, are you including the implications for cash, people, and risk? Are you measuring progress against organizational goals consistently and communicating that back to decision makers? All of this can help demonstrate value and progress into a more complete IT

Maturity Model, the details of which will be outlined in a later chapter.

For our purposes here, thinking along these lines can help determine the blend of cloud computing solution you employ, and thinking it through with the business goals in mind will ensure your input is valued when the decision makers are mulling the sales pitch from service providers. In our experience as consultants, decision makers often have an entrepreneurial mindset, and are making tons of decisions on the fly. This means they don't always take the time to solicit comprehensive feedback to inform decisions, whether company direction, hiring, and goals. The more you are able to initiate conversations that are both value and data-driven, the better. Squeaky wheel gets the grease? You better believe it!

Chapter 8

But Weekends Are For More Work, Right?

Ah, weekends. Firing up the grill. Tossing around the old pigskin. Guac and chips on the coffee table, ready for the game. You didn't spend top dollar on that NFL package for nothing, right? How's that fantasy league coming? In point of fact, if you're a semi-successful IT director, none of what I've just wrote will make any sense to you whatsoever. It might as well be in ancient Sanskrit. You probably haven't had a free and clear weekend since somewhere around that unforgettable Windows 95 release party.

It's become almost axiomatic in certain IT circles that you are unemployable if you insist on your weekends. Weekends simply mean more work. Ok, Ok, IT people are probably more interested in testing their homemade robot than a fantasy football league, but you never know. The point remains: others are walking their dogs, going to yoga, or taking their paycheck to Whole Foods for that tasty organic fenugreek and quinoa salad (the secret is the tarragon. Yum.), while you work on your pallor in the home office in the basement if you're lucky (the actual office if you're not), checking patches for clients, getting to backlogged work. Since much backlog work consists of literal logging of work done, the pun here is intended.

If you don't have complete control, with the ever changing threats to the security of your network, if you don't have solid processes in place for risk assessment, automated notifications, a chain of communication, and dare I say it, an emergency communication plan, if you are short on process, you're more than likely long on weekend work. If you have a voice mail from your old dungeon master asking what's become of you, you know exactly what I'm talking about.

Lack of robust process leads to overwork, whether this manifests itself in overtime, late nights, all-nighters, or weekends patching the servers, either way, enough is enough. While every IT department may need a rotating on-call schedule, depending on your client base and your SLAs, there should be a happy work-life balance as well. It doesn't have to be all stress, all the time. The IT Maturity Model can help you out here.

 Let's get a little more down and dirty with the IT Maturity Model to get a better picture of how it can benefit you. First, let's look at the term maturity itself. No we're not talking about MS DOS or your Sega Genesis collecting dust in the basement, we're talking about a professional mindset. For our purposes, **IT maturity is the measure of how well your technology supports the efficiency and productivity of your organization in fulfilling its mission, vision, and business goals**. As the kids used to say, whoomp, there it is. This involves thinking strategically and proactively, not ad hoc and reactively. Doing this allows your organization to see you as an asset to strategic planning, not just involved in a series of projects and purchases. If you are not employing technology to engage, anticipate needs, understand business flow, purchasing patterns, and ultimately to increase revenue, you are not maximizing your potential. We hope you get on board the IT Maturity Model before your CEO does, let's put it that way.

Today's IT tools provide means of increasing agility, and of consolidation and integration over sprawl. Think of the possibilities in having your entire website, sales, publications, marketing, mobile website, apps, and ticketing service all in sync, all providing analytics data to improve decision making at each level. Today's IT tools can do that. As businesses grow, so does service sprawl, and even online efforts fall into silos and become fragmented. Next Gen IT can synthesize, integrate, and coordinate the disparate. Think of the four domains of organizational IT: *network, online components, data,* and *management,* all working in unison with coordinated principles to deliver on the mission, vision, and objectives. That's IT Maturity.

Let's also take a look at a means of categorizing clients on a spectrum of IT Maturity Model adoption. **Our four basic categories for IT Maturity are Limited, Functional, Effective,** **and Mature**. In the *Limited* stage, companies are often stuck with outdated legacy hardware that is long overdue for an upgrade. Often at this stage, the components are not even necessarily all compatible and integrated coherently. Employees store and maintain their own records, resulting in inaccurate data for both internal and client information at multiple levels. The network is slow and virus laden. The web site design is not mobile compatible and results in difficult navigation for many users. There is no content management system in place for web site content, and any marketing initiative is detached from other organizational developments. Training on effective use of technology is lacking. Employees accept the limitations, often grumbling about how difficult it is to find information and get things accomplished. At this stage, the success of the organization relies in great measure on individual employees slogging through.

The *Functional* stage includes improved technology but with limited integration and automation. For many employees, access is an issue, and there are several points in the system creating bottlenecks with unnecessary access restriction. There is inconsistent communication with clients, including mixed messages from different sources, with much time still wasted acquiring accurate information. Few people in the company have access to data from anywhere, anytime, across multiple devices. Mobile use is still difficult, although the hardware is up to date, and network uptime is strong. Targeted communication is still lacking and training is spotty. There is some web site integration, minimal strategic planning in support of overall organizational goals, and a general lack of structure.

In the *Effective* stage, the IT department is more than a functional tool and a huge drain on operational resources. It supports the overall vision, mission, and objectives of the organization in an integrated way. There is both macro and micro level planning and strategy with the IT budget. There is some amount of social media awareness and interaction among clients. The infrastructure is up to date, perhaps integrated with some form of cloud solution for high availability across devices from anywhere. Data is stored in central databases, integrated across departments, whether ticketing service, CRM database, marketing tools, or client communications, all driven by mission, vision, values, and up-to-date organizational objectives. There are established policies, procedures, and processes for delivering service and internal communication. The network is secure and outages are few and far between. Members have a single sign-on for integrated use, rather than logging into each new application. All media efforts are integrated and aligned with overall strategic goals. Communication is fresh, relevant, coordinated, and targeted to specific potential client segments. Strategies are evaluated and updated in an ongoing, consistent way.

IT Maturity. Shangrila. Nirvana. Transcendence. We've arrived. I'll wait while you pat yourself on the back. Done? Got it. Moving on. In the *Mature* stage we put our integrated system to use, both in meeting current needs through coherent, strategically aligned processes and procedures, but also in putting data analytics to use to anticipate future needs, and plan solutions and adjust budgets to optimize system performance and maximize impact to both current and potential clients. Rather than seeking out solutions and implementing them to address needs and get out of the red, the IT department shows forward thinking and innovation in services offered and means of delivery. The IT departments becomes an integral part of strategic planning across the board, helping employees think of client needs and how to address them in an efficient way, rather than narrowly focused on their own role or departmental goals; people have the bigger picture in mind at all times given the widespread integration of all systems. Strategies and high levels of service are clearly defined and measured, up-to-date business intelligence informs strategy, new technology and solutions can be integrated seamlessly, since their arrival is anticipated and planned for. In short, IT becomes a consulting role within the organization, helping drive decision making to a high degree. All tools, processes, and people are integrated and pursuing a unified goal that is clearly defined. That's IT Maturity.

If you need to take a breath, we understand. It takes thoughtful planning, strategy, and multiple points of input to get something as complex as an IT department, of whatever size, unified and integrated. This starts with identifying goals for the IT department itself. It's here, at this key point of expanding your sense of what the IT department can do within the organization that makes a huge difference. Yes, you need execution. Yes, you need a strategy. But first, you have to expand your vision of what IT can bring to the table, and commit to performing that role within the organization. Internalizing that sense of ownership of the role of strategic driver of business objectives can make a palpable difference and solidify your value. Once that belief and some solid processes and systems are in place, you can fire up the grill, break out the cooler, and get the hammock out of storage. Enjoy a hard earned weekend with automated systems, integration, and security alerts in place. You don't have to micromanage a well-planned system. That's not a guarantee there will never be an outage, that you'll never work overtime, obviously, but wouldn't it be gratifying to know that would be the exception, rather than the norm, and you may be able to plan a relaxing stroll through the Saturday farmer's market on the search for those tasty tangelos that come around every so often.

Chapter 9

Right, But Where's My Raise?

So, let's review for a moment. You're in IT. You're overworked and underappreciated. And that could change. How? By shifting to an IT Maturity Model. This shift requires several steps. First, you need to have a clear understanding of the company's current business goals, which are usually broken down on an annual, quarterly, and monthly basis. If you're not in on meetings where these are frequently discussed and where their knowledge is assumed, getting to know them may require a meeting or two with key decision makers. Even initiating on this level can earn some points. Maybe you say you'd like to conduct an IT Maturity Assessment and measure progress against organizational goals. That may initiate a change in the way in which decision makers communicate with you and the type of information you're included on. With three to five key goals in mind, identify the main pain points or obstacles to achieving those goals. Once you have that, assess the way in which your current IT environment, processes, and procedures is set to become a driver in meeting those goals, or addressing the pain points. Maybe the ROI on integrating a cloud adoption model, integrating systems and allowing constant access and productivity jumps out right away. Maybe other changes are needed, whether in personnel, solution consolidation, escalation options, or outsourcing. The answers are there.

Putting processes and procedures in place with system automation in all key areas, including networking, security, emergency management, storage, and analytics means you don't need to work on the weekend. Next Gen hardware, applications, and cloud adoption should be seen as tools, as strategies, as pieces of the overall picture of moving toward an IT Maturity Model. Now let's say you take the step, develop a Maturity Model plan, establish realistic timelines, implement metrics, and track progress. You've developed measurable IT driven ROI for the company. With automation in place, you've freed up your weekends, you've let go of the reins a little bit, adopting a collaborative mindset over command and control. Great. Things are humming.

At this point, we're thinking beyond job security and increased time on your hands. Now we're looking at a raise. When it comes to raises, requests are often ill informed, driven by personal need or perceived workload. Instead, you do well to focus on measurable ROI. C-level executives are thinking in terms of the bottom line, asking themselves "how much spend generates how much revenue?" We might take care to dot the "i" and cross the "t" for every project, work overtime, talk down an outraged client, go the extra mile time and again, give up weekends, and so on. And while your boss likely realizes you're a reliable worker on some level, they're also nose deep in balance sheets, trying to make the numbers work for the company. So you make it easier for them to give the go ahead on a raise if you do the legwork and crunch the numbers ahead of time and demonstrate the value proposition in dollars and cents. If you know how the business works, and have good processes in place, your raise isn't going to come from cloud, from updates on hardware, patches, or even a new certification. It's going to come from how efficiently IT is running relative to business needs. The extent to which you're able to put into practice the steps outlined above will help you articulate how you're supporting business growth or needs from financial perspective, regardless of how much control you maintain or how elaborate your time sheet is.

Instead, consider how IT is supporting business initiatives with true metrics attached. Can you cut operational costs by reducing inefficiencies through automated workflows and processes? By how much? What is the associated savings amount on a monthly basis? Can you cut the project lifecycle through automated handoffs? How much time is currently being wasted? Running some numbers on who is doing what job may be worthwhile.

Here's a quick example of how a profit assessment can help make personnel decisions. Let's say you're spending half your time handling tier 1 and tier 2 problems, fixing printers, cables, and, say, system updates. If you're making 6K a month, and your assistant is making, say 3K month, that's a total IT salary spend of 9K. At 50% of your time and 100% of your assistant's time handling tier 1 and 2, that means those issues are eating up 6K a month. If you added a second assistant, allowing you to stay virtually free and clear of tier 1 and 2 issues, yes, that would bump total IT salary spend to 12K a month. But if you could demonstrate that with that freed up time, you could implement systems to cut costs for the company by 8K-10K, you've not only paid for the extra position, you've possible earned a bump yourself. These could be automated notifications preventing downtime, automated handoffs between work groups, increased network access and productivity, and so on. Adopting the Maturity Model, if you moved toward predictive analytics, marketing, sales, and internal processes alignment, as well as marketing demographic targeting methods with a measurable impact on conversions and sales, you may not only cut costs by 8K-10K, but realized additional profit for the company. Let's be conservative and say the new conversions lead to 1K growth a month. Over time that can very significant for an SMB! Going through this process will depend on your current IT department, your internal organization, your organizational goals, your current IT infrastructure etc. What we're advocating with the IT Maturity Model is simply that you add a set of lenses through which to look at your current situation. Given your reality, it may mean your staff model changes, but whatever your current income as IT manager, you can add to it *and* add value to the company by thinking more globally about using some of these tools available.

Now we can go back to some of the current issues we're seeing with IT managers and address these as well. Many IT managers in companies of all sizes across all industries tend to narrowly view their value in terms of system integrity and security. They adopt the command and control mindset because they see their value in these narrow terms, thinking if they aren't perceived as being in control, they won't be viewed as necessary, and therefore become superfluous or redundant. But if you could articulate security, backups, and efficiency as part of Maturity Model, removing the need to maintain the appearance of control, you could demonstrate true, measurable value that is not fear driven, neither for the company, nor for yourself.

Making that shift can jump start productivity for yourself, for your department, and for the company as a whole. And the issue of a raise will take care of itself. Well, you may need to send an email and shake a hand or two. We also recommend for the raise conversation, depending on your relationship to the executives, that you ditch the threadbare polo from the 2001 tech conference and don something more befitting a person of your current (or at least desired) stature, a polo from, say, the 2011 conference would even be better!

Now that we've taken a look at demonstrating value for your company using the IT Maturity mindset, let's consider the role of IT from a Maturity perspective in the context of current discussions in the field and perhaps challenge some of the accepted wisdom.

Chapter 10

Yep, It's Another Gartner Quadrant Discussion

Whoa, Nelly! Don't get me started on Gartner Quadrants, now. I'll be jabberin' away til the sun comes up. Why, I'm so enchanted by the quadrant, I might call it *magic*. Assuming you haven't been inundated with Magic Quadrant information, this is a fancy-shmancy way of analyzing a particular company and assessing it according to set criteria that situates the company in one of four quadrants: *Niche Players*, *Challengers*, *Visionaries*, and *Leaders*. Gartner identifies the x axis continuum as the company's "completeness of vision," and the y axis as the company's "ability to execute."

A quick google search can help illustrate the point, but the company's position on a Gartner Magic Quadrant chart will change based on the service under analysis. So, for example, for Business Intelligence, say, Microsoft would be in the leader quadrant (as of the time of this writing, mind you), with SAP a challenger, and Actuate a niche player. If the service under analysis is unified communications as a service, say, then Microsoft is now a challenger, with ShoreTel a leader, and AT&T a niche player. Make sense? Got it. Moving on.

The Service Driven Cloud

Quadrants can be helpful to make investment decisions, gauge market trends over time, conduct forecasts, etc. Ultimately, of course, the analysis provides only a snapshot at the point in time at which the assessment is conducted. Gartner does a good job of assessing strengths and concerns regarding companies, their product sets, and their market position, but for our purposes in advocating an IT Maturity Model with the inevitable cloud service component, the Quadrant model analysis is severely limited.

It is helpful to gauge what products are in the quadrant, but we'd like to suggest that beyond compatibility, private, public, or hybrid models, and industry forecasts of AWS' market position, for the IT director, what really matters is *service delivery*. Whether it's custom configuration of network, application layer support, infrastructure design, implementation, and consultation, partnerships with high SLAs, what matters is the end user experience. What matters are the services that enable mission critical applications, however customized the need is, to maintain high functionality.

The idea of the *Service Driven Cloud* is the cloud component of the IT Maturity Model. With the business and tech hats both within reach as you sit at your desk, the Stetson and the Fedora, if you will, we perceive that the out of box functionality for different types of cloud computing services are less important in and of themselves than the services wrapped around and delivered with them. That's where we've found a huge value add for our customers. Not in Amazon over VMware cloud, of private over hybrid necessarily, although those considerations come into play, but rather in the level of trust we build through excellent service delivery and ensuring the end users experience is a smooth one.

That doesn't mean problems never arise, but when they do, there need to be processes and procedures in place as we've discussed, with an emphasis on excellence of customer care. Many of the big boy cloud providers have simply decided staffing to the extent necessary to provide excellent services isn't scalable according to their business model. That leaves the value added resellers (VARs) and managed service providers (MSPs) to pick up much of the slack there and provide tailored services for specific vertical industries. If you're in healthcare, for example, there are specific platforms, applications, and guidelines that require an increasingly large amount of high level expertise. If you're main clients are in architecture, or law, or semiconductors, or education, there will be slight variation and nuance in your specific service needs, even though the out of box cloud hosting options remain the same.

The Service Driven Cloud, then, refers to both the set of services wrapped around cloud hosting and delivery, _and_ the excellence with which that service is delivered. A service driven approach combines great services with excellent service. Quality services are proactive, tailored, innovative, responsive to actual client needs in the field, and maximize the benefits of cloud computing, such as security, agility, and efficiency for your industry in general and your business needs in particular.

Now, we all know what great service is in the consumer space, but what about from a managed service provider? Great service here means attentive, timely interaction with high service levels, consistent customer care from all levels of your provider, with a consultant mind-set that maintains close contact with the client, going beyond a break-fix model by developing new solutions corresponding to client goals at any given time with specific metrics in place. This is far more than fixing the printer linked to the network. With this in mind, we free up IT to become a business driver.

If we keep this in mind, we allow ourselves to pursue to client's best interest, rather than a Gartner Quadrant label. We remain focused on service, identifying road maps for achieving business goals through technology deployments. This allows IT departments to hone in on relevant skills to refine, certifications to pursue, and personnel to hire.

On a basic level, cloud computing itself requires a shift in thinking, just like the utility electricity model required a shift in thinking around the turn of the century, as we mentioned earlier. In those early days of electricity, shops and warehouses and factories had to supply their own electricity, which was expensive and resource draining. At some point, other companies had the idea to generate electricity in a central location, provide it as a utility with permanent availability as long as you patched into the grid. Today, we take it for granted. At the time, though, it was a pretty big deal. In cloud computing terms, that constant availability means your organization's functionality is no longer bound to one location. Virtualization with hosted desktops, for example, means your entire integrated network, with documentation access, mission critical software, and communications applications can be accessed in same state from anywhere with a simple login, with standard performance, compute, storage, and security. Think of this as a baseline benefit. A standard, if you will. By now, if you're in IT, you've had your brain wrapped around this for some time, even if the boss doesn't want to upgrade the 2003 legacy server that's been outdated for the past two refresh cycles (ahem).

In consulting with a wide array of companies and performing cloud readiness assessments, these macro level terms like efficiency, agility, and security are often too vague for some business owners, especially in the SMB sector, since they're focused on refining their value proposition and developing their own 60 second pitch. Wrapping their head around cloud computing, let alone IT Maturity, and thinking through the benefits on a granular level is not in their wheelhouse. With that in mind, let's take a look at a few cloud benefits with a tiny bit more specificity. Remember, adopting the IT Maturity Model means thinking beyond the basic benefits of IT and cloud. To leverage it fully, and to provide that inside perspective, you have to understand something of how your business works at a micro level as well. Without that understanding, the cloud becomes just another under-utilized tool in the tool box.

Adopting a **virtualization solution** can help improve performance and productivity for established companies, but it makes a ton of sense for a startup without physical offices just yet, providing system integration, shared documentation, corporate communication apps like Yammer, cloud based Software Suites like Office 365, etc. With a skeleton crew of 3-5 in a startup, and, say, 2 or 3 contractors used on occasion, with just a few mission critical applications, but some high security needs a startup might have would make virtualization a perfect fit here, especially with any expectation of growth. It just scales extremely simply. For the established IT director, the value is just as clear: managing a complicated organizational infrastructure can be reduced to a single console, with patches, updates, downtime and reboots, passwords and permissions all centrally managed. Huzzah!

For the newbies, getting rolling in any market requires honing in on your mission, vision, brand, brand narrative, marketing message, 60 second pitch, value proposition; however you want to word it, you need it. It's a fast paced market out there with a ton of competition. Naturally, mission and vision are valuable to ensuring you stay consistent internally and so everybody knows what they're pursuing. Managing the external message is equally important.

What does this have to do with cloud computing solutions? Glad you asked. Cloud computing platforms have helped marketers envision simple, streamlined ways to manage marketing campaigns. Rather than just writing up some copy and sending it out with fingers crossed, cloud based platforms like MS Dynamics CRM, Constant Contact, or Hubspot allow far more integrated approaches, allowing users to build, manage, measure, and revise marketing campaigns to targeted audiences. Copy, social media outlets, corresponding campaigns, landing pages, leads, conversions, and interactive analytics are all integrated from a central application.

At the Fortune 500 level, chances are some form of these solutions are already in place. Why, you ask? Well, sir, the big boy software developers pursue these other big fish companies with proof of concept presentations early on in the process, not just to get the big account, but also to establish market presence and brand centrality. Hey, I'd do it, too! With your Mature IT hat on, having already wrapped your head around central focus, practice, and business goals for your organization, providing some options with pricing attached along with a stab at possible savings can reinforce your identity as a proactive IT manager, not just a back-end break-fix mechanic.

If your business operates from multiple locations, which is increasingly the case, whether or not you have a central office, the cloud solution that makes a lot of sense is virtual desktop infrastructure (VDI). This provides the traditional benefits of cloud computing in general, with offsite servers, reducing opex and capex by cutting server and software upgrade, updates, and maintenance. The secure connection provides access to organizational data, applications, and corporate email. It can also extend the life of workstation hardware, since the compute, storage, and networking needs aren't dependent on the physical workstation, but really more on the bandwidth, which is all part of an initial cloud readiness assessment anyway.

VDI makes sense for larger organizations with the need for standard access to particular applications, data, and features, with offsite productivity. Some cloud hosting providers are upping the ante here by shrink wrapping the whole kit and caboodle: they have partnerships with Google, Dell, and whomever else to provide an end to end IT solution for the organization. They meet with you to consult, draw up a network plan, provide any desktops or thin clients you may need "free of charge," meaning the leasing price for the hardware is rolled into hosting costs (or *amortized*). Once this gets some traction and proves effective for large organizations, we predict this will be fairly standard practice, given the cost savings, and zero hardware cost involved. The pricing tends to be calculated based on a per-seat or a per-average-user per-month basis, rather than the amount of licenses, applications, or usage, making it a fairly affordable option over traditional legacy server network infrastructures.

Again, some IT managers get a slight uptick in anxiety when these offers get pitched, since they assume it makes them redundant. That's where the IT Maturity Model comes in handy: with a knowledge of the deep structure of your organizations goals, targets, functioning, and needs, you're still needed to help steer the ship, only now, you don't have to build it, too.

Maybe the most obvious benefit of cloud computing is in the area of security and failover. Usually, by now, vendors have systems in place with comprehensive redundancy, multiple data centers, and top notch failover solutions, whether software defined like Veeam and Zerto, that provide continuous replication solutions, or otherwise.

Finally, we are seeing a huge upward trend in a new kind of malware called ransomware. These little buggers have carved out a little niche, in which they attack your system through ads or attachments, sounding innocuous enough like, hey it's Fedex and we have a package for you. A co-worker clicks on the attachment and whammo, you've got a cryptolock virus attacking and locking down files. Here's the fun part: unlike those old spam emails from other countries, claiming you've got $50000 in unclaimed funds waiting if you just send the $5000 now, these hackers are asking for $300 to release your system. They're like pirates, only if pirates let you go for a few measly doubloons, but could board about a 100 ships a day. A few successes have emboldened the hackers, and we see this as an upward trend. A virtual desktop infrastructure means it's possible to reconfigure file sharing, root access, and permissions in such a way to limit the damage, all fairly simply. On top of that, there are more robust malware detection and prevention solutions beyond your standard anti-virus software. All this is far more easily implemented and monitored with a virtual infrastructure.

Yet another area of benefit derived from cloud computing is in business management tools. These are ever increasing, but are intended to allow organizational IT departments to build, buy, manage, and refine cloud services to find the sweet spot of investment of resources and productivity. These services like Cloudability and Atmosphere, provide cloud cost analytics, usage, productivity, and optimizations reports, helping to identify and eliminate inefficiencies. They can also help monitor adherence to governance and security policies, which goes hand in hand with our emphasis on procedures and policies above. Sometimes you develop policies, email them out, or walk the workforce through them in a kick off presentation, and still it doesn't stick. The good boys and girls rail against lack of accountability for the bad apples who gum up the works. These cloud tools can help ensure that accountability is more easily achieved with monitoring software. Customize the workflow tracker and get flagged if something isn't implemented or documented correctly, and prepare a standard tongue-lashing for the worst offenders! Services like these can be especially valuable if an infrastructure is spread across multiple cloud and on-premise infrastructures, serving as a kind of meta-cloud integration service across platforms.

Another cloud based platform gaining a lot of traction is HR management. Let's say you're in growth mode and need to fire up the HR, but, um, unfortunately you don't really have an HR department, and everybody is already working beyond capacity, which is the whole reason you need to fire up the HR. It's pickle, no question. Short of fleshing out a department, one option to go with is an HR solution like HR Cloud, and admittedly easy name to remember for a cloud based HR solution. This suite offers the ability for accomplishing both internal and external HR tasks. What are you core service offerings? What are the core skills required at each position? What are key performance indicators per position? Performance monitoring, onboarding, training tools, and business documentation tools all make these a huge benefit, especially for small business with low Opex budgets (Jack Nicholson voice: "Is there another kind?") They can also provide employee feedback loops, standard employee reports, skills assessment and cloning for future hires at that position, and so on. This can help solve another problem for companies without an HR department, which is inconsistent metrics, inconsistent nomenclature, documentation, storage location, etc. It keeps the process standardized and organized. That's no small selling point for small companies that waste time and productivity simply searching for an old form.

The transition to the cloud is underscored by Microsoft CEO Satya Nadella's announcement of the company's increasing focus on cloud-based platforms. Google is fleshing out its Google Drive suite for enterprises. Amazon's AWS is growing by leaps and bounds. Enterprise IT spend is shunting heavily into cloud platforms, services, and applications. We've pretty much already hit the tipping point here with business's cloud focus. Even in the Managed Services sphere, we're seeing businesses hardest hit by the 2008 market crash are those who did not plan for cloud computing options, since, in the wake of everyone tightening their budget, this became an increasingly attractive option to companies.

In providing some different options for cloud based services, we're not really advertising the cloud. Big companies like IBM, Amazon, and CenturyLink do that already. They have much bigger advertising budgets, anyway. The word is out. It's coming, like it or not. The question is how to position yourself within your organization to leverage cloud resources and services to the advantage of your company, to stay proactive and maintain status as a forward thinker. The cloud is the least of your problems, it's a means to an end, part of a Mature IT approach. They key for IT managers is to have a deep understanding of their business needs, and to develop mature solutions addressing those needs, including any relevant cloud or managed service solutions.

Circling back to the Gartner Quadrants, I'm wondering, are you a leader, a niche player, a visionary? No, you're a problem solver, but unlike Vanilla Ice in his heyday, you're a proactive problem solver, understanding needs, making sense of the available data for informed decisions and recommendations on the best way for your company to deliver its service in a competitive market.

In all that hubbub, where does the managed service provider like us come in to the picture? We serve as consultants, helping you match your business needs to the right technology, design, and implementation. Our biggest customers see our value add as freeing them up to focus on end user needs at a high level, addressing the sticky business problems. We have specialists augmenting the service delivery component and wrap services around the utility of cloud computing. We address all back end issues from Tier 1 through Tier 3 with helpdesk personnel and field techs working with high service level agreements. We've got that part covered like it ain't no thang.

Rather than dealing with printers, network cables, AD and password issues, we want you to be the onsite expert where technology meets your business needs. Whether you have the title or not, we want you to become the company CIO. We want you to become your company's best technology consultant, drawing on our expertise as a third party resource. What this means is you no longer have to sweat the small stuff. If you engage with a managed services provider like us, and you're sitting around the office after hours on a Friday, then it's more than likely you have some attachment issues.

Breathe. Let go. It's going to be ok.

What it means is you didn't give your managed service provider a call. You didn't create the ticket. You didn't let go of the command and control mindset, you didn't adopt an IT Maturity Model. For shame! Don't sweat the small stuff. In fact, with the extra time on your hands, go to the mall, buy a Cinnabon, swing by the bookstore and buy a copy of *Don't Sweat the Small Stuff*.

You're a consultant now. It's time to think creatively. And to do so, studies show you need a change of pace, enter into a new space (like a perfectly air conditioned mall complete with cinnamon roll scented food court. Ah!). You go ahead and let the managed service provider handle the little stuff, whether a Tier 1 onsite issue, a Tier 2 permission and access issue, or a Tier 3 coding issue. Kick back, open a cooler, whittle the letters C-I-O into a sign for your office door. Go ahead. Get yourself some Mature IT. Life's short.

Enjoy it a while you can.

ABOUT THE AUTHORS

Matt Murren has worked as a security consultant and IT engineer for General Electric, as well as providing business and health care IT consulting to a variety of companies, from SMB to Fortune 500. In 2001, he co-founded True North ITG as a means of providing enterprise level IT solutions to small-to-midsize businesses. Since then, the business has experienced steady growth, with annual revenue 40% above the average Managed Services Provider. Matt has overseen the expansion of True North beyond original managed services to include health care IT, cloud hosting, cloud consulting and software-defined data center services to clients of all sizes nationwide. He resides with his family in Lake Stevens, WA.

Marc Shaw has worked as an educator and consultant in both public and private sectors, conducting training for management and administration, specializing in the areas of instructional strategies, branding, marketing, and organizational communication. Most recently he has served as both Communications Manager, Business Analyst, and Story Architect for True North ITG. He resides with his family San Diego, CA.

www.ingramcontent.com/pod-product-compliance
Lightning Source LLC
Chambersburg PA
CBHW051210050326
40689CB00008B/1260